Epic

Bugatti Chiron

JULIA GARSTECKI AND ANDREW DERKOVITZ

BLACK
RABBIT
BOOKS

Bolt is published by Black Rabbit Books
P.O. Box 3263, Mankato, Minnesota, 56002.
www.blackrabbitbooks.com
Copyright © 2020 Black Rabbit Books

Marysa Storm, editor; Catherine Cates,
interior designer; Grant Gould, cover designer;
Omay Ayres, photo researcher

Library of Congress Cataloging-in-Publication Data
Names: Garstecki, Julia, author. | Derkovitz, Andrew, author.
Title: Bugatti Chiron / by Julia Garstecki and Andrew Derkovitz.
Description: Mankato, Minnesota : Black Rabbit Books, [2020] | Series: Bolt.
Epic cars | Includes bibliographical references and index. | Audience: Ages 9-12. |
Audience: Grades 4 to 6.
Identifiers: LCCN 2018018006 (print) | LCCN 2018019258 (ebook) |
ISBN 9781680728415 (e-book) | ISBN 9781680728330 (library binding) |
ISBN 9781644660324 (paperback)
Subjects: LCSH: Chiron automobile–Juvenile literature.
Classification: LCC TL215.C535 (ebook) | LCC TL215.C535 .G37 2020 (print) |
DDC 629.222/2-dc23
LC record available at https://lccn.loc.gov/2018018006

Printed in the United States. 1/19

Image Credits

Alamy: Ricky Deacon, 6–7;
bugatti.com: Bugatti Automobiles,
Cover, 1, 11, 14–15, 19 (bkgd), 20–21
(btm), 23, 24, 26; bugattihistory.com:
Bugatti Automobiles, 3; commons.wikimedia.
org: Heinz Reutersberg, 13; geekreview.org: Top
Car Reviews, 4–5; images-free.net: Unknown, 16
(top); commons.wikimedia.org: Alexander Migl,
32, 31; medialounge.bugatti: Bugatti Automobiles,
8–9; Newscom: Bugatti/Cover Images/, 28–29;
Shutterstock: Alexei Zatevakhin, 12; bestv, 19 (jug);
Elenamiv, Cover (bkgd); Jia Li, 20–21 (top); Miro
Vrlik Photography, 27; Tom Grundy, 16 (btm);
venuechilton.com: DEADMAU5 CARS, 26–27
Every effort has been made to contact
copyright holders for material reproduced in
this book. Any omissions will be rectified
in subsequent printings if notice is
given to the publisher.

Contents

CHAPTER 1

Racing Down
the Road. 4

CHAPTER 2

Design. 10

CHAPTER 3

Power and
Performance. 18

CHAPTER 4

An Epic Car. 29

Other Resources. 30

Racing

Down the Road

The Bugatti Chiron looks like a sculpture. It has a powerful, smooth body. But the supercar isn't just beautiful. It's strong. It screams to 62 miles (100 kilometers) per hour in less than 2.5 seconds. Other cars don't stand a chance. They're left in the dust.

An Amazing Car

Bugatti first showed off the Chiron in 2016. Its look amazed people. And its 1,500 metric **horsepower** stunned them. The Chiron costs millions of dollars. But people say it's worth the price. They say the car has the best design money can buy.

The price can easily reach more than $3 million.

WING

SMOOTH SHAPE

NARROW
HEADLIGHTS

GRILLE

VENTS

CHAPTER 2

Design

No car looks quite like the Chiron. Bugatti designed it for speed. Its body moves air around and through the car. The back end's shape reduces **drag**. As the car changes speed, flaps near the front wheels move. The flaps adjust **downforce**.

The Chiron went through more than 300 hours of wind tunnel testing. The tests showed how air hit the car while driving.

The Chiron's body is carbon fiber.
Carbon fiber is very tough but light.
Less of the material is needed to
make the car safe and strong.

Designed to Use Air

The Chiron's brakes and engine
work hard. They produce a lot of heat.
Designers gave the Chiron vents to
cool them. Vents bring in fresh air.
Even the headlights double as vents.
They guide air to the front brakes.

The Interior

Inside, the design is simple. Most new cars have touch screens. But the Chiron doesn't. Bugatti knows technology changes quickly. Within years, technology can become outdated. It can leave a car looking old. Electronics can take away a car's beauty too. Designers wanted owners to focus on driving.

The car has a stereo system developed just for Bugatti.

Chiron

One buyer wanted an alligator-skin interior. Designers put alligator skin on his car's dash.

Personalized

Bugatti offers 31 colors for the car's leather interior. But Bugatti makes each Chiron specifically for each customer. If customers want special colors, Bugatti makes sure they get them.

CHAPTER 3

Power and Performance

The Chiron's engine is just as impressive as its design. A quad-**turbo** 8-liter W-16 engine gives the car its incredible power. Thanks to this massive engine, the Chiron can **accelerate** quickly. Its top speed is 261 miles (420 km) per hour.

Running at Top Performance

The Chiron needs a lot of air and water to run properly.

211 ···▶

gallons
(800 liters)

AMOUNT OF

WATER

**PUMPED THROUGH
THE ENGINE
EACH MINUTE**

10
number
of radiators

more than
15,850
gallons
(60,000 l)

**AMOUNT OF AIR USED
BY THE COOLING
SYSTEM EACH MINUTE**

CHIRON VS. VEYRON

Before the Chiron, Bugatti released the Veyron. The Chiron is faster and more powerful.

Chiron

METRIC HORSEPOWER
1,500

0 TO 62 MILES
(100 KM) PER HOUR
less than
2.5
SECONDS

TOP SPEED
261
MILES
(420 KM)
PER HOUR

Veyron 16.4
Grand Sport Vitesse

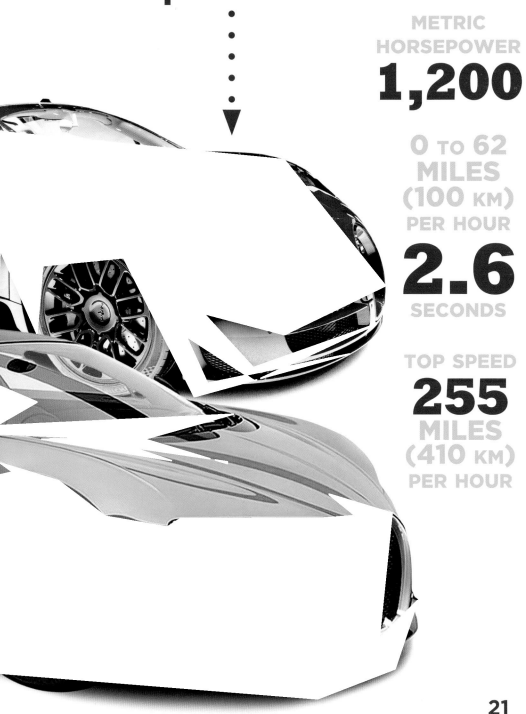

METRIC
HORSEPOWER

1,200

0 TO 62
MILES
(100 KM)
PER HOUR

2.6
SECONDS

TOP SPEED

255
MILES
(410 KM)
PER HOUR

Brakes

Fast cars need powerful brakes. The Chiron's brakes are big. They are larger and thicker than the Veyron's. But they don't weigh as much. They're made from carbon silicon carbide. This material is light but strong. Heat shields cover the tops of the brakes. They push away heat to keep the brakes from **overheating**.

• •

The Chiron's rear wing changes position based on speed. At times, it acts as an air brake.

BRAKE

Drivers use a different key
to go into Top Speed mode.
The mode lets the car reach
its highest speed.

Driving Modes

Drivers can change more than just the cars' looks. They can choose how the cars drive. The Chiron has five driving modes. Each mode changes the car's settings. The body of the car can raise or lower. Steering and **stability** can also be changed. Certain choices let the driver **drift**.

By the Numbers

2

TOTAL SEATING

80.2 INCHES
(204 CENTIMETERS) WIDTH

178.9
INCHES
(454 CM)
LENGTH

47.7
INCHES
(121 CM)
HEIGHT

500

TOTAL NUMBER OF CHIRONS BUGATTI PLANS TO MAKE

$2,998,000

BASE PRICE

An

Bugatti doesn't rush to make its cars. Each Chiron is individually designed. They are powerful pieces of art. It's easy to see why so many people love them.

accelerate (ak-SEL-uh-reyt)—to gain speed

downforce (doun-FAWRS)—a force that increases the stability of a motor vehicle by pressing it downward

drag (DRAYG)—something that makes action or progress slower or more difficult

drift (DRIFT)—to break traction with the back of the car and slide through a curve

grille (GRIL)—a metal frame at the front of a car

horsepower (HORS-pow-uhr)—a unit used to measure the power of engines

overheat (oh-vur-HET)—to become too hot

radiator (RAY-de-ay-tuhr)—a device used to keep the engine of a vehicle from getting too hot

stability (stuh-BIL-i-tee)—being able to remain steady and stable

turbo (TUR-bo)—a device that helps an engine increase power; turbo is short for turbocharger.

BOOKS

Bodensteiner, Peter. *Supercars.* Gearhead Garage. Mankato, MN: Black Rabbit Books, 2017.

Fishman, Jon M. *Cool Sports Cars.* Awesome Rides. Minneapolis: Lerner Publications, 2019.

Oachs, Emily Rose. *Bugatti Chiron.* Car Crazy. Minneapolis: Bellwether Media, Inc., 2018.

WEBSITES

Bugatti Chiron
www.bugatti.com/chiron/

Bugatti Chiron
www.caranddriver.com/bugatti/chiron

BUGATTI Chiron 0-400-0 km/h in 42 seconds – A WORLD RECORD
www.youtube.com/watch?v=PkkV1vLHUvQ

INDEX

A

acceleration, 4, 18, 20

B

brakes, 13, 22

C

carbon fiber, 12

cooling, 13, 19, 22

costs, 7, 27

D

designs, 4, 7, 8–9, 10,
    14, 16, 17, 22,
    26–27, 29

driving modes, 24, 25

E

engines, 13, 18, 19

H

horsepower, 7, 20

S

speeds, 18, 20, 24